WORKBOOK

For

HOW TO WIN FRIENDS AND INFLUENCE PEOPLE

The Only Book you Need to Lead you to Success

Dale Carnegie

HAPPY Publishers

ISBN: 978-1-950171-89-7

Table of Contents

How to Use this Workbook For Enhance Application

Complete beginners can begin using this Workbook for How to Win Friends and Influence People: The Only Book you Need to Lead you to Success By **Dale Carnegie** to get immediate help of the major lessons and Summary of this book.

The goal of this Workbook is to help even the newest readers to begin applying major lessons from How to Win Friends and Influence People: The Only Book you need to lead you to Success By **Dale Carnegie**. Results have shown us that learning is retained better through repeated real-life applications

By using this Workbook, readers will find Summary and Lessons which we believed were major in defining the crucial messages of the author in the book.

There are Spaces to jot down your answers to lesson at the end of each Section. Take out a pencil, pen, or whatever digital technology you would put to use to jot down, implement, and make happen.

And don't forget to have fun - While at it. This Workbook Will Teach you to go after your goals, how to win people to yourself and achieve your maximum potential.

About the author

Dale Carnegie is known as one of the most famous writers ever to walk the earth. From a young age, he developed a knack to correctly pass knowledge to others and inspire them to be a better version of themselves, which explains why he was able to get a full house at the first attempt at public speaking in 1916 and how he slowly built up a profile that is revered ever since.

He has several books which have all recorded astounding success all over the world with millions of copies sold. "How to win friends and influence people" is considered his most famous book and has become a pacesetter in human social relations, transcending time to remain relevant.

Introduction

From the first page, Dale Carnegie's book "how to win friends and influence people is a masterpiece that has been in print for over 75 years and is still very relevant in the world today. To achieve this level of consistency is no mean feat, and after going through this workbook, we shall find out why that is so.

This workbook is a simple guide to the points raised in the book itself and how to apply them in real life. This work would help you develop a greater sense of human relations and how to improve better your social skills and understanding of how to get the best out of people without sweating much.

Furthermore, you would be able to pause at intervals and take notes of the progress being made at that point, preparing yourself for the next chapter.

Let us begin.

Part one

Fundamental techniques in handling people

Chapter one

If you want to gather honey, don't kick out the beehive

There is a prevalent belief among several criminals in America's history about being misunderstood. The likes of "Two Gun" Crowley, Al Capone and Dutch Schultz all gave voice to their belief that they were good men whose good side demonstrates the inability to harm people yet were hunted down for one crime or the other. These guys were confirmed murderers. It begs the question, why hardened criminals chose to sing a different tune after being captured?

Astonishingly, the reason for this manner of behavior is the fact that a high number of humans detest taking criticism for what they had done, instead would focus on giving explanations while regretting being caught, not the deed itself. The author puts the number at ninety-nine times out of a hundred. A person is likely to get into a defensive mode when criticized. This scenario generally hurts their pride and seek to humiliate them in some cases, hence the vigorous attempt at playing down the weight of their actions.

You would find out that more often than not, criticism does not fix human relationships in the long run. It might lead to instant fear which could bring about immediate improvement, yet does nothing to get to the root of the main issue at hand. For this to happen, understanding and dialogue must be present in an attempt to discover what the underlying factor is before attempting a solution.

Ultimately, you would discover that in all manner of human interaction, people are quick to point the finger on others but less inclined to blame themselves for their actions. The author describes criticism as homing pigeons, which would always come back home after flying around for a while.

This lesson was learned in real time by Abraham Lincoln, who at a stage in his life, publicly wrote letters to mock and insult people he thought their actions undesirable. These letters gained him, several followers. Then came to the turn of a fellow named James shield who didn't take the scathing criticism too kindly and challenged the former to a fight to the death which thankfully didn't proceed, and taught Lincoln a valuable lesson that perhaps, such public outbursts weren't much fun and he subsequently resorted to treating people with compassion.

For parents who are quick to dish out criticism to the young at the slightest provocation, well, kindly take a few moments to go through *father forgets*- an all-encompassing note which has been reprinted over and again and translated into several foreign languages. The message therein would more likely give you a different perspective on how to better handle certain situations without setting off a time bomb.

Lessons

- Several people tend to focus on positives, instead of accepting their wrongdoings
- Things can always get out of hand when you choose to criticize others
- Treating people with compassion works better and is a longer lasting solution as against the quick fix which criticism might bring.

- Don't be in a hurry to criticize, complain or condemn others at all times

Goals

1. In a few word, write down why you should desist from criticisms?

____

____

____

____

____

____

2. Moving forward, what is the best way to relate with people?

____

____

____

____

____

____

____

3. How best can you deal with the young ones?

____

____

Action steps

- Always keep in mind, the possible futility of being eager to criticize people as they could immediately take a defensive stance and have things escalate quickly
- As a person, it is okay to accept your faults without feeling the need to cover them up, this is the first step to recovery
- Be kind in your dealings henceforth, compassion is a better tool to use at all times rather than brashness

Chapter Two

The big secret to dealing with people

There are two ways to get people to do what you want. The first is by making them want to get it done and the second which isn't without complaints is by coercing them either by using force or threatening to. While the former comes with better options and brings long term results, the latter is simply a small fix that could lead to a cascade of issues much later. Before taking up either option, you need to ask yourself what exactly it is you want and are trying to achieve through your choice.

Notable are the basics of life which include food, shelter, and clothing, with almost everything else dispensable for a period. There is one other thing which is commonly craved by many people- the need to feel important. More often than not, we seek to be recognized and stand out in all dealings with other people. This situation is perfectly natural and is one factor that separates humans from animals.

It is this innate desire to feel important that led a lowly grocery store attendant who was uneducated to read a few law books, turning out to become a president of the USA- Abraham Lincoln was his name. This desire has also led to the invention of so many of the world's technology and companies. Works of art aren't left out, as the likes of Charles Dickens was inspired to write outstanding novels and Sir Christopher Wren to design his symphonies in stone.

On the other hand, people feign being lesser citizens in an attempt to get the sympathies of others and in turn, gain some level of relevance and importance. On the extreme, several people have been known to go crazy simply because they felt neglected and reveled in the attention they got afterward.

From the above stated, it becomes clear that people would always seek a level of importance to be attached to them. This situation makes the ability to make people feel important, a valuable asset in human relationships. It does not matter that that person might be a subordinate. If you can make them feel important, then they are more likely inclined to do what you want.

Lessons

- There are two significant ways to get people singing to your tune. The choice on which method to employ solely rests on you.
- Everyone wants to feel important
- People go to specific lengths to get the needed relevance.
- Being able to give people that feeling of importance means you can get them to do what you want without hassles.

Goals

1. Which necessities do you carve most?

____

____

____

____

2. How do you wish to get that feeling of importance?

3. What method would you employ in getting people to do what you want and why?

Action steps

- A decision is to be made on what method you are to employ in the quest to become an important member of the society
- While the necessities of life are actually vital, being relevant can help you achieve them as you wish. The plan is to constantly stay that way.

- Henceforth, make an effort to have people around feel essential, as this would place you in an excellent position to have them do things for you willingly
- Do not hesitate to give sincere appreciation when needed

Chapter three

He Who Can Do This Has the Whole World with Him. He Who Cannot Walks a Lonely Way

For the most part, we tend to focus on what we want while attempting to get other people to do things for us. Has it occurred to you that there would be better results if you take time to find out what they want and use it to bait them into doing what you want? Thereby staying in control all along and determining what happens and when.

Since birth, everything you have ever wanted comes from the feeling of desiring that thing. If that feeling is strong enough, you seek what you want and are ready to exchange valuables such as money for getting them. If it weren't that important, perhaps you would not spend your money in trying to get it.

The art of persuasion is one that has worked wonders over time and has been employed by all manner of people in subtly getting what they want. For this to be successful, you need to relate well with the person.

It isn't just about making an effort to get someone to do what you want. Find a way to make them do things on their own free will. Once you have found a way, other factors fall into place. Persuasion entails free will on both sides, hence the need to be observant in identifying what is needed to get the whole process over the line.

According to Henry Ford, "If there is any one secret of success, it lies in the ability to get the other person's point of view and see things from that person's angle as well as from your own."

This scenario would allow you to weigh both sides and decide how best to proceed without losing sight of the important.

The real test of service is in the ability to put yourself in another's shoes in an attempt to feel like they do and better relate with their situation. Unfortunately, this act is one that several people never get to embrace in their lifetime but has been known to reward the few that do richly. There is no better way to persuade someone than to show them that you understand what they are going through.

Lessons

- Being able to persuade people successfully goes a long way in determining how much they are willing to do for you
- The surest way to get them to do things for you is by showing that you can relate with them on a reasonable level and care as well.
- It's perfectly natural to want something. Being able to get that without trampling on others is an excellent ability.

Goals

1. What impression would you rather leave in the quest to persuade people?

____

____

____

____

____

2. What method would you use in persuading people?

3. Can you honestly make effort to serve others as stated above?

Action steps

- Understand the importance of service as a means of getting in the good books of people in the long run and make it a habit today

- When in need of something, determine how valuable it is at that point, then decide how much you want it and what you are willing to exchange for it.
- Do not hesitate to listen to other people. It is a way of learning what their situation is, thus putting you in good stead to decipher what is needed to get them on your side.
- By doing the above mentioned, you are willingly arousing the other person's interest in doing what you want out of their own free will.

Part two

Six ways to make people like you

Chapter four

Do this, and you'll be Welcome Anywhere

While going through life, there is that possibility of trying to make people like you. It is a great idea, yet one that would most like fail, not because you are unlikable but simply because people care more about themselves than they could ever care for you. Once this process has registered in your mind, the plan changes from trying to get people to like you, to improving yourself further.

By developing an interest in the activities of others, there is a better chance of developing and sustaining a warm friendship which comes through mutual interests. It is the best kind because the effort at maintaining the relationship would come from both sides and not the initiator bearing the brunt.

To win and keep friends, you must go out of your way to invest time and interest in the life of others, which goes a long way in laying a strong foundation that is a lot deeper than the surface level friendships which seems to have become common in the world today. Imagine having someone you talk with on a casual note, yet you go the extra mile of finding out their birthday and wishing them well on said day. Don't you think such a gesture would leave a lasting impression?

There isn't much more to be said, a great way of moving from the point of being acquainted with good friends is by showing sufficient interest in their life, and makes it easier, as it would take so much effort for a person to pretend through this process. The chances of building a genuine friendship are impressively high.

Lessons

- Show genuine interest in the life of others.
- While not straightforward at times, building a friendship from scratch is a rewarding proposition for everyone involved.
- Instead of making futile attempts at getting people to like you, make yourself better as a person and show the needed humility by being keenly interested in their life.

Goals

1. Identify someone you want to be friends with, what do you know about them?

____

____

____

____

____

____

____

2. How do you intend showing interest in their life?

____

____

3. How will you sustain the friendship?

Action steps

- To be interested in the life, take time to find out what their situation is. This would help when trying to figure out what their interests are.
- Be sure to have a few interests in common. It would significantly increase the possibility of having lots of topics to talk about and real activities to do together.
- Become genuinely interested; this is important.

Chapter five

A Simple Way to Make a Good First Impression

A first impression they say lasts forever. That is often the case as people are more inclined to keep in mind, your countenance at the first time of interaction. If your goal is to make an excellent first impression, keep in mind that while people may wow at your outfit and jewelry, the real deal breaker that would have left them very impressed is the look on your face. That is what they would most likely remember.

For instance, the smile of a baby melts even the strongest of hearts, same as your dog which practically jumps as high as it can in joy to welcome you back home after a few hours of separation. No matter how tired you are, it is possible that you'll appreciate the affection first and think of other things later, and has happened because of that outward smile and glee.

The effect a smile has on people is amazing. Most employers would prefer to employ an intern who smiles often and has a great personality to handle the reception area than a veteran with many years of experience who rarely smiles. This choice can be pinned down at the image they wish to project to clients and the general public. The smile is also a way of expressing to your employer that you are having a swell time doing your job, which shows you are better inclined to be more productive at it.

William Steinhardt, a broker, recounts his own experience with smiling. During the early phase of adulthood and marriage, he hardly ever smiled at anyone or anything. His wife, who was already used to this manner of behavior, got the shock of her life when her husband one day smiled at her while greeting in the morning. Seeing the effect, it had on her and other people, William now made it a habit to smile at everyone that he comes across, thus noticing that they smile back. The mood in his home and environment significantly improved after making an effort to learn this one habit.

Medical practitioners have said it time and again that it takes way more muscles to frown than to smile, which means that while you break into that smile, your facial muscles tend to relax and your personality radiates good vibes. People are more inclined to have a conversation with you with a smile on your face.

Most times, happiness comes from your thought. It isn't who you are or what you are doing that can make you happy, but the multiple things you are thinking about at that moment, hence the need to keep the best memories at the top of your subconscious, you might break into a smile for no reason while walking on the road.

Lessons

- The best first impression comes with a huge smile plastered across your face
- A smile generally shows how pleasant a person you are and encourages others to approach you
- A smile can get you that better job you have been craving
- Make a conscious effort to always think about the right things; those are most likely to encourage a smile out of you even when you would rather not.

Goals

1. What could you gain by smiling more?

2. Are there things you could lose by keeping a straight face at all times?

3. How can you ensure to keep a smile on your face always?

Action steps

- Having seen the benefits of smiling all the time, ensure to wear one at all times.
- When in doubt, stand before a mirror to see just how better you look with a smile on your face
- When meeting someone, ensure to smile at them. It encourages them, defusing any tension that might have been around you.
- A smile costs nothing but creates much; you have nothing to lose by wearing one at all times.

Chapter six

If You Don't Do This, You Are Headed for Trouble

An awe-inspiring ability which would continuously help you in relating better with people is by remembering their first name. It is never the easiest thing to learn, but one which should be practiced over time and perfected.

Jim Farley best illustrates this; a man with little formal education but started as a salesman, mastering the names of everyone he came in contact with, thus elevating their status when he meets with them later and correctly calls their first name. When asked, Jim opined that he could remember the first names of over fifty thousand persons and this was no joke.

He did this by enquiring for the full name of the people he came in contact with, with a little background information about their family and work. Once this happens, he creates a safe archive in his mind, which would enable him to remember these details next time he meets the person.

This particular ability endeared him to several people and came to light when he became the campaign head for President Roosevelt. He could send letters to thousands of people, starting with their first name and ending with his. There is no better way of showing a person's relevance than by recalling necessary information about them, not minding how long ago you came by this info. Impressive.

Furthermore, Andrew Carnegie, who is known as the king of steel, hardly knew anything about steel, yet successfully ran his business. He had hundreds of people who were more knowledgeable, work in his company happily. This fact was due to the little detail that he knew everyone's first name and made an effort to socialize whenever he came across a member of his staff.

The gentlemen mentioned above were able to achieve extraordinary levels of human relationship by mastering the art of giving relevance to people, no matter who. While many people would not see the need to make any effort at all, they were consistent, hence liked and respected by all. Another factor that helped was that they pronounced these names in full without seeing the need to either shorten or mispronounce in any way.

Lessons

- It doesn't matter their social status or origin; everyone craves importance and respects who gives it to them.
- Being able to call people by their first name does you no harm at all. On the contrary, it increases your value to them
- While calling people by their names, remember not to mispronounce it as this might be seen as disrespectful

Goals

1. How do you intend to remember everyone's name?

____

____

____

2. Would it be possible to not make any mistakes while pronouncing any name?

3. What do you hope to achieve by perfecting this ability?

Action steps

- While meeting with someone for the first time, make effort at asking for their name and any other information that would help you always remember.

- Once the name is known, try to always keep the correct pronunciation in mind at all times.
- Comprehend the significance of perfecting this skill and do it in style.
- Always have in mind, there is no name more critical to a person than theirs.

Chapter seven

An Easy Way to Become a Good Conversationalist

The trick of having a good conversation isn't by being the talker or a half listener. It is by showing the person you are talking to that they have your utmost attention and you are very much interested in the topic at hand. For example, you meet an accomplished formula1 driver at an event. After exchanging pleasantries, you can start by telling him how fascinated you are by what he does and watch him go on a narrative about the cars they drive and the race as a whole.

All you need do is the occasional head nod to show you are following, a smile on your face and steady eye contact. He could talk for hours on end, and you would not only gain valuable insight but are more likely to get acquainted adequately after this. From the above, you hardly said anything during the entire conversation but made a good conversationalist.

When asked, a top interviewer shared an essential insight on scaling through interviews unscathed. This scenario, he said, can be achieved, giving the interviewer all the attention while a question is asked. They feel respected and are better inclined to provide you with favorable consideration.

For business owners, spending a fortune to redecorate your store for greater appeal is quite noble. It does not necessarily guarantee more people would come in. Employing cheerful clerks who are great listeners is one way to ensure customer satisfaction, because the customers love attention and having salespersons that listen to them attentively with a smile naturally does a lot to lift the mood around and encourages them always to come back.

A great way to disarm a volatile person is by giving them attention. When riled, further acts of confrontation only serves to heighten tensions, while a soft smile accompanied by steady nods and appropriate remarks would slowly remove the negatives, further bringing calm to an otherwise dicey situation. Most people get to calm down when you aren't returning their fire with fire but are patiently nudging them towards being calm by paying full attention and elevating their importance.

Lessons

- A good conversation requires the full attention of the listener to encourage the speaker
- Lasting impressions are made by how well you listen when spoken to
- Situations can be properly defused by listening
- Do not be in a hurry to talk all the time. Just giving someone your full attention is all it requires to be a good conversationalist

Goals

1. How can you become a better conversationalist?

____

____

____

____

____

2. In an interview, how can you ensure a batter chance at success?

3. What can be done to calm a situation?

Action steps

- To make great impressions around people, listen to them when they speak
- Do not let your attention wander when being talked to. This can be hugely disrespectful and embarrassing.

- When someone is upset, take the less traveled route of listening to their grievances, speaking when necessary.
- Being a great listener means you encourage others to talk about themselves while you give unwavering attention with a genuine smile.

Chapter eight

How to Interest People

President Roosevelt is considered a people person in most quarters. One of the most endearing qualities in his arsenal is the ability to carry on a conversation with his visitors who are visiting for the first time, in a manner that might suggest they have met before. The key to achieving this is quite straightforward. All the president does is to take a look at the interests of the intending visitor a night before their arrival, taking to heart the things they care about while building a conversation around those subjects.

Being in the presence of the president and hear him talk about horse racing or automobiles which you have a keen interest for is a welcome surprise. Not many things can be quite as disarming. It gives you the feeling of being famous for having the president go through all that trouble while automatically placing you in a position to be more welcoming and perhaps charitable in the long run.

Before meeting a famous person, kindly take time to find out what their interests are. It will make for a more interesting conversation if you demonstrate your ability to know these things beforehand. They are more likely to be receptive when you talk about things they are interested in.

Lessons

- Taking time to learn the interests of people before meeting them puts you in an excellent position to get a proper audience.

- When speaking with people, steer the conversation to topics that would be beneficial to them one way or another.

Goals

1. How do you hope to impress an important guest?

____

____

____

____

____

____

2. What are the gains of carrying out this research beforehand?

____

____

____

____

____

____

Action steps

- Develop the habit of being adequately prepared before an important meeting, it does a world of good. Always talk in terms of the other person's interest
- Seeing the benefits that come with developing this habit, ensure to make it a part of your skillset

Chapter Nine

How to Make People Like You Instantly

This particular endeavor is one which is immensely beneficial to both parties immediately and In the long run. It is neither rocket science nor quantum physics and happens by giving an honest compliment about one thing or the other you genuinely like about the person.

For instance, a person having a bad day is more likely to cheer up when you say hi with a smile and tell them that you like their jacket or hair with all honesty. Once they see that you mean it, a huge weight would be off their shoulders, and they would smile back at you and generally have a better day.

Such compliments should be well thought out and expressed genuinely. It would be bittersweet to tell someone you like their bald spot or their fake teeth. This process requires tact and observation and might be a bit difficult if you are meeting the person for the first time. The better thing would be to take a little time and have an honest assessment, intently focused on finding a few positives to compliment.

On average, humans are selfish and only care about themselves and loved ones. While this isn't ideal, it makes it even better for the person who you are sending a compliment, as they would feel special to be appreciated by you who might be a total stranger, and goes further to show that they have your approval and have gained some form of worth from the endearing words you have said to them.

Away from the compliments, there is another way to make people like you instantly, and that is by using adjectives like 'sorry' and 'thank you' appropriately. After serving your drink, saying a quick thank you immediately tells the waiter that you are a nice person who isn't condescending not minding the nature of his job. He would be better positioned to attend to you swiftly the next time you come around. People hardly ever forget such pleasant encounters.

Lessons

- The right words could be the difference between a great and terrible first encounter
- Do not rush to throw kind words, be sure the words are on point and deliver them honestly
- Appreciating people endears you to them instantly.
- Do not overlook the importance of saying sorry and thank you amongst others.

Goals

1. When meeting someone for the first time, what is the first thing you do?

____

____

____

____

____

2. What are the appropriate word to use?

____

____

Action steps

- Once you meet someone, make the required effort to find the best things to appreciate about them
- Before saying a word, do well to plaster a pleasant smile on your face.
- People can be sensitive about these things, endeavor to say what you have in mind with honesty.

Part three

How to Win People to Your Way of Thinking

Chapter ten

You can't win an argument

In public, it is quite easy to get someone to like you instantly, same way it is easier to get disliked on the spot. Comporting yourself is most likely to win you the admiration of all present while acts of lousiness would seek to achieve the opposite. For instance, being in a social function means you get to meet people from all classes of society. Once a topic comes up, openly challenging the speaker would do your chances no favors as the consensus would be that you are making efforts to embarrass the fellow.

No matter how right you might feel about your opinion, merely nodding with a smile would reduce the chances of a public confrontation. Of course, you can always seek the person out later and give your view, which shows you respect them all round and is bound to gain you their respect and gratitude as well. You can't go wrong with this.

According to Abraham Lincoln, "No man who is resolved to make the most of himself, can spare time for personal contention." Constantly engaging in arguments always end with a perceived winner and a massively bruised ego. While this might not matter to several persons, it is a sure way to continually pit yourself against people while creating the impression of being a troublesome fellow.

Lessons

- Arguments do little to help you; public showdowns are even worse.
- Your reputation would be considerably tainted if you are known to always argue in public
- Airing your opinions in private earn you massive respect from your audience

Goals

1. While in public, how do you coordinate yourself?

____

____

____

____

____

____

2. What benefit are there to arguing publicly?

____

____

____

____

____

____

Action steps

- Kindly restrain yourself from arguing in public, no matter who is involved.
- If you disagree with an opinion, smile and take mental notes to deliver to the speaker in private
- While making your point, do not feel the need to ridicule. Your tone and approach matter a lot.

Chapter eleven

A Sure Way of Making Enemies—and How to Avoid It

In a bid to prove your superiority whether in knowledge or otherwise, most people end up trying to enforce their will on others. Man is a rational being who would resist individual attempts at subjugation out of pride or to save face, which entails that if you wish to change a person's opinion or do something to convince them, it should be done subtly while the results are made public, and does not involve telling people they were wrong.

Also, realizing when you are wrong and admitting to it is an attribute that can never go wrong. No matter what the situation may be, this single act can swing the pendulum in your favor and help to avoid making an enemy- on the other hand, refusing to admit your fault when wrong is a sure way of making a few enemies.

In the heat of an argument, stopping to admit wrongdoing would automatically thaw the ice in that environment by many degrees, as people are going to listen to what you have to say at this point, which means that you must show value to the opinions of others without telling the person is wrong and causing some form of embarrassment.

Lessons

- It does not pay to tell someone their opinion is wrong openly. They might end up resenting you.
- When in doubt, always ensure to keep quiet.
- Acknowledging your wrong does a lot more good than you can imagine.

Goals

1. What could happen if you openly accuse someone of being wrong?

____

____

____

____

____

____

2. What effect can admitting your wrongdoing have on a conversation?

____

____

____

____

____

Action steps

- Always have in mind what happens when you accuse someone of being wrong
- To get away from dicey situations, endeavor to admit when you are wrong
- People want to know that they matter. Do not cause a rift by being blinded with your desire to appear correct at all times.

Chapter Twelve

A Drop of Honey

How we approach things and issues goes a long way in determining what the outcome would be. Pulling out your gun with a hand on the trigger would most likely get a similar response from the other person, while a genuine smile accompanied by kind words and dialogue would meet the same energy. When meeting with an enraged person or group of people, words, and actions must be chosen carefully to avoid escalating the situation even further.

There is an old saying which opines that "a drop of honey catches more flies than a gallon of gall." Which means that if you extend a hand of friendship, there is a higher chance of being received well. People automatically respond in kind to the manner of vibe coming from others within same environment.

For business executives, the way you handle any form of inconvenience at the workplace can determine the outcome. For instance, if your workers are seriously demanding an increase in wages, it might not be the best time to act brashly as the ripple effects never end. Instead, it would make better sense to extend an arm of friendship which would be returned in kind while a suitable solution for both parties goes on.

Lessons

- It pays to begin any conversation in a friendly tone
- In human encounters, what you give is what you are more likely to get
- Different scenarios calls for diverse manner of approach all in bid for better understanding

Goals

1. How best would you handle a confrontation?

____

____

____

____

____

2. While talking to aggrieved subordinates, what is the best tone to employ?

____

____

____

____

____

____

Action steps

- Make a mental note to always extend a hand of friendship first.
- Once the situation is calmer, do not relent in being friendly.
- Always begin in a friendly way.

Chapter thirteen

The secret of Socrates

On average, several people look forward to interactions where they would display a level of superiority to others. This behavior comes from the need to always focus more on our areas of strength, thereby attempting to put a cloak of inferiority over the other person. Most people don't take too kindly to this and would immediately start to build up some form of resentment over you which might spill over at a later date.

Being able to get someone saying yes from the onset of a conversation helps the chances of them liking you, which means that you are talking about things in which there are mutual interest and understanding for, instead of showing off what you know, and they do not.

On the other hand, getting 'No' for an answer implies rejection, which isn't on the list of needed attributes to excel in the art of getting people to like you. Getting a positive response is a simple yet efficient technique which puts you in an excellent position to get something meaningful from that conversation.

As the Chinese say, "He who treads softly goes far."

Lessons

- Do not feel the need to show off, no matter how better knowledgeable you might be
- A great way of ensuring mutual likeness is by getting people to willingly say yes to you, even if you just met.
- Taking the right steps improves your standing with people.

Goals

1. How would you go about having people say yes to you?

____

____

____

____

____

2. While in the midst of people, what is the first step you should, take?

____

____

____

____

____

Action steps

- A smile can never go wrong
- No matter the social setting, take the right step by talking about common interests
- Get the other person to say yes right from the start by choosing the right words.

Chapter Fourteen

A Formula That Will Work Wonders for You

There is always the possibility that the other person is wrong. Instead of laying blames like many people would, take the unusual step of attempting to understand why they believe or act that way. This knowledge would come in crucial and can even help you develop a baseline and get to know what kind of person they are.

Have in mind that every person has a different thought process coupled with diverse ways of understanding and processing things. This situation is not the time to criticize; the effort should go towards genuinely putting yourself in their shoes as it would help you come to terms as to why people reason that way. Seeing things through another person's eye has short and long term effects, which ultimately leads to mutual understanding and smoother resolution of conflicts instead of chaos.

People feel at ease when you cease from lashing out at them even if it is justified. Having a heart talk where you make it evident that you aim to understand rather than criticize, makes people open up and trust you, feeling that you genuinely care. People come toward positive energy.

Lessons

- Continually try to see things from their perspective
- There are reasons why certain people behave in a way. It is a pattern which can be known if you pay close attention
- Never be in a hurry to display superiority. A little humility and understanding would work better here.

Goals

1. How do you react when someone thinks differently from you?

____

____

____

____

____

2. Once you discover a behavioral pattern, what is next?

____

____

____

____

____

Action steps

- Pay attention when someone is speaking their mind, it could help you understand their way of thinking even better.
- If in doubt, ask a few questions to get a better perspective
- Try honestly to see things from their perspective, no matter how different it may be from yours.

Chapter Fifteen

What Everyone Wants

Ideally, it would be wonderful to have a particular phrase or method that would end arguments and have people listen when you speak. There is such a phrase, and it goes thus "I don't blame you one iota for feeling as you do. If I were you, I would undoubtedly feel just as you do". Such a response immediately arrests any situation, no matter how fiery it was.

Amongst other things, such answer, correctly carries the message that you do not blame the other person for their reaction since it is on their perception and perhaps temperament, and you would most likely react in the same manner if you were in their body. On the general, this suggests sympathy, and that is one emotion that a high number of persons on earth do not reject.

By showing sympathy, it becomes easier to win over your audience since you have demonstrated human capacity to relate with their current predicament. People automatically see you as kin and are obliged to listen further to what you have to say or, including viable solutions.

Lessons

- Be sympathetic to everyone's situation and desires
- By showing sympathy, you slowly warm into the other person's heart
- It also shows how kind you are, ultimately seeing a quick resolution of conflicts.

Goals

1. When faced with a temperamental fellow, what do you do?

____

____

____

____

____

____

2. What other gains are there to showing sympathy?

____

____

____

____

____

Action steps

- Always listen to people, that way it would be easier to show sympathy
- When faced with a difficult situation, endeavor to show the other person you value their opinion
- Ultimately, display a level of kindness that would warm the heart of others.

Chapter Sixteen

The Movies Do It. TV Does It, Why Don't You Do It?

Speaking the truth is noble and always the right way to go, yet the world has advanced to a level that the truth should come with flair. You stand a bigger chance of capturing the minds of all who come across it, which is why the media accompany news with vivid images and motion pictures so real that people have to stop and listen.

The next time you are telling the truth about something, do well to pack it with necessary details to become a more attractive prospect for your audience, which would ensure that they imagine what you are talking about, thereby creating a solid mental picture which they can always refer back to when needed.

Take, for instance, a marriage proposal, which could be done by whispering to your partner and handing them a ring to suit the purpose. It becomes an elaborate and sometimes mind-blowing experience by going down on your knees before popping the question. While they may say yes with the former pattern, the latter creates a lasting memory, capturing their attention in an instant to give you the right environment to carry on.

A significant reason why children books are so elaborate with pages accompanied by multiple colors is that kids are usually bored with several things, one being dull words and pages. Hence the need to brighten up the message with the right image and several colors that would ensure they remain interested for as long as it takes.

Lessons

- The truth should not be a dull affair, as there are better ways of making it more attractive to your audience.
- While directly speaking can get someone to look up, the real method to genuinely get their undivided attention is by displaying flair.
- Doing the above shows, you value their attention and have gone through the process of grabbing it with both hands.

Goals

1. Now that you know, what must be done the next time you are passing a message?

____

____

____

____

____

2. On the long run, how do you intend adding the dramatic when passing a message?

____

____

____

____

____

Action steps

- Before going ahead to pass a message, have a plan on how to make it more colorful
- Do not look down on the occasion, every time is a good time to do as you have learnt.
- Pay attention to what is need to spice up your message at every different situation.

Chapter Seventeen

When Nothing Else Works, Try This

Ever thought of ways to inspire an underperforming bunch? The answer is simple- a good old competition which seeks to increase the desire to excel. It is not an attempt at pitching one against the other, but a solid effort towards raising the competitiveness amongst them by having one side do slightly better, thus indirectly nudging the other side to beat that mark.

Once a gauntlet has been thrown down, the nature of man to always excel among his peers would immediately kick in, with the drive to buckle up and make better attempts at succeeding. Without proper challenge, it might be difficult to get people out of their comfort zone, which can be particularly frustrating and even dangerous at the place of work.

You would discover that situations where threats, coercion, and even persuasion has failed, laying down a feasible challenge might save the business with minimum casualties. At times, you may not know what you can achieve or how far you can go until the right motivation is laid down. The heights you might be able to reach albeit quite easily would amaze you as tasks which were once considered extremely difficult won't be seen in that light anymore.

Lessons

- When trying to get people to be more productive, throw down the gauntlet
- the goal isn't to make people direct rivals but to inspire each side to do better

- When a challenge comes to, your limits will stretch, and you will be able to scale new heights.

Goals

1. How do you intend to motivate a group of people to do better?

____

____

____

____

____

2. When in competition, are you willing to excel?

____

____

____

____

____

Action steps

- When in need of motivation, find healthy competition
- Take note of the progress being made
- Ensure that everything is fair

Part Four

Be a Leader: How to Change People without Giving Offense or Arousing Resentment

Chapter Eighteen

If You Must Find Fault, This Is the Way to Begin

There is never an easy way to criticize or critique another. The blow is often unexpected and most likely taken in bad faith. The proper way to deliver your opinion is by preparing the person for a soft landing, thereby reducing the effects of your words or actions.

The first step to achieving this is by finding something positive to say, like a nice haircut or a beautiful dress to put the person at ease and get a smile from them before going on to drop your remarks, just like a barber lathering a man's head first before proceeding the barb.

For instance, staff may write a report on which you noticed a few errors. Laying into the person out of the blue is not the best idea. You could start by praising the parts where they did a good job, getting them to feel good before pointing out areas where they need to work on, and you would find out that the person would be eager to make the necessary corrections in record time.

On the other hand, you could bring mistakes to their notice without being direct about it. This method is mostly successful because the person gets the right feeling that you are trying to correct them without being demeaning in any way.

Lessons

- Start with the good points before shifting to the bad

- The plan is to offer a reprieve with a solid chance at redemption
- If done correctly, the person would have their pride intact and would be willing to go to any length for you.

Goals

1. How best can you deliver bad news?

____

____

____

____

____

2. What do you hope to achieve in the above named scenario?

____

____

____

____

Action steps

- A genuine compliment always settle nerves, start with that
- Once delivered, do not go extreme by being harsh, simply point out what can be done better.
- Ultimately, have in mind the benefits of getting this right.
- Always begin with praise and genuine appreciation.
- If possible, call their attention to the issue indirectly.

Chapter Nineteen

Talk about Your Own Mistakes First

It's always easy to point the finger at others, often forgetting our issues at that time. For instance, laying the blame on a young secretary though they are performing much better than you did at that age is never a great approach. For starters, you must have gained the needed skills through years of experience, which makes it unfair to be that harsh on others with significantly less experience than you.

To put this in perspective, pointing out your own mistakes which might have been way worse at that age would go a long way in assuring them that this is a learning curve and they aren't doing a terrible job. For beginners, making isolated errors is part of the work process and is necessary to gain the confidence and skills needed to excel just like you someday. Putting them at ease makes it easier to relax and pay attention to what they need to learn.

Being able to admit your mistakes, encourages others to work hard to fix theirs. While you may not make similar errors presently, speaking of when you made similar or worse ones goes a long way in describing you as humane and willing to teach

Lessons

- There is no better way to point out mistakes than by talking about yours
- Talking about yours makes others understand that your motive is to educate and not to chastise.

- People would be at ease around you once you show that side of you.

Goals

1. When someone makes an error and is terrified, what should you do?

____

____

____

____

____

2. What is the aim of talking about your past mistakes?

____

____

____

____

____

Action steps

- Seeing as the person is already upset at their error, your manner of approach would either fix or escalate the situation
- Talking about your mistakes should not be in a cocky tone.
- The plan is to show genuine concern while attempting to teach, do not show off.

Chapter Twenty

No One Likes to Take Orders

As the title suggests, being renowned for barking out orders at all-time can become tiring and gets people to fear rather than respect you. While the latter might be ideal for several business owners, it does not bode well for anyone who seek to get liked by others.

Instead of always reeling out orders authoritatively, making suggestion always get people to see things from your point of view and see why you might think that way. Once that has registered, they are better inclined to keep an open mind while considering your opinion and learn a few things from you.

Rather than say "Do this or do that," or "Don't do this or don't do that." you can say "You might consider this," or "Do you think that would work?"

Again, it would make better sense to ask the right questions to find out the whole story, thus giving a better grasp of the situation to enable you provide the correct suggestion to solve whatever issue there might be, allowing them to save face without having to get a further battering from you

Lessons

- Never be in a hurry to give orders, ask relevant questions first
- Instead of giving orders, make suggestions
- Suggestions would provide people with a chance to learn from you instead of fretting at your orders.

Goals

1. When faced with an error from a subordinate, what should you do?

____

____

____

____

____

2. What would they stand to gain from your sincerest suggestions?

____

____

____

____

____

Action steps

- No matter how upsetting the situation might be, do have in mind that you stand to gain more by subtly offering suggestions than giving fiery orders.
- The goal remains to teach. That should be done in a conducive environment which aggressive behavior such as always giving out orders cannot provide
- Whenever you feel like giving orders, ask questions first and get a grip on the situation
- Let the other person save face

Chapter Twenty-One

How to Spur People On to Success

To further motivate people, it is always great to look at the progress they have made in recent time and praise them, which would naturally spur them to continue on that path of growth and self-improvement while their output increases further. This technique has been used on animals for centuries and can work correctly on humans.

People value recognition, which is what they would get once you acknowledge how far they have come while encouraging them to improve further and is always a morale booster that goes a long way in enhancing the esteem levels and self-belief amongst people around you.

Have in mind, the fact that abilities blossom when watered with praise but do the exact opposite when shrouded in criticism. You are not only improving conditions all around you by doing the former; it gives people sufficient room to grow.

Lessons

- For people around you to do better, do well to praise them when needed.
- Encouraging those around you gives them room to do better
- When praised, the environment becomes better suited for better performance.

Goals

1. What effects would encouragement have on people around you?

2. On the average, what do you seek to achieve by being pleasant?

Action steps

- Take into consideration, the effects of encouragement both the persons and the environment as a whole
- When in doubt, take stock on how far they have come and what good your praises has done.

Chapter Twenty-Two

Making People Glad to Do What You Want

One way to get people doing your will is by making them feel too significant for a particular role, hence creating an opening to maneuver as you wish. This technique requires tact and the ability to use the right words. Once they are adequately calm, a proper opportunity would come up, which would not involve looking over your shoulder.

On the other hand, this method can be used to get what you want without upsetting the other party. Say, for example, you as a singer, people you share close affiliation with get to invite you to perform all the time and do not wish to go, how best to proceed?

It's simple. Send thoughts on how honored you feel to have been invited by them but regrettably announce that you would not be able to come and declare a substitute singer. By so doing, you have successfully turned them down graciously while solving what would have been a problem with your absence.

From the above, you have made the best of prickly situations which could have turned out much worse. There is no better way to make people do what you want than this.

Lessons

- You can get what you want without stepping on toes
- It is possible to turn people down with much grace
- Making people feel important can feed their ego and give the needed opening to make changes subtly.

Goals

1. Is it important to keep their ego intact while making your move?

____

____

____

____

____

2. Ultimately, what do you hope to achieve?

____

____

____

____

____

Action steps

- This technique must be gotten right, hence the need to get your facts right before making a move
- Choosing the right words is essential while attempting to get people to do as you want

Conclusion

This workbook aims to sufficiently expose you to the salient points raised in the book under review. While not a substitute for the comprehensive work itself, suitable mention occurs and questions answered with the need for proper reflection as you turn the pages.

If followed accordingly, there is an excellent chance of learning what is vital in an attempt to make friends and influence people. For a greater understanding, total focus is recommended to make for easier reading and the ability to grasp what is in the pages.

Other Recommended WorkBooks

You are a Badass Workbook >> ISBN: 1950171868

WORKBOOK for The Longevity Paradox>>

ISBN: 1950171795

A JOURNAL For Becoming | A Gratitude & Self Journal (Becoming By Michelle Obama Quotes)>>

ISBN: 1098520211

A JOURNAL For Daring Greatly>>

ISBN: 195017185X

A Journal The Subtle Art of Not Giving a F*ck>>

ISBN: 1950171833

WORKBOOK for The Subtle Art of Not Giving A F*ck >> ISBN: 1950171779

WORKBOOK for Eat To Beat Disease >>

ISBN: 1950171809

44413782R00044

Made in the USA
Lexington, KY
10 July 2019